YOUR LAND
AND
MY LAND
The Middle
East

We Visit

AFGHANISTAN

WITHDRAWN

Tamra

Orr

Mitchell Lane

PUBLISHERS

P.O. Box 196
Hockessin, Delaware 19707

Visit
AFGHANISTAN

SYRIA

Beirut
LEBANON ★

Haifa
ISRAEL
Jerusalem ★

US

Dead Se

YOUR LAND
AND
MY LAND
The Middle East

Afghanistan
Iran
Iraq
Israel
Kuwait
Oman
Pakistan
Saudi Arabia
Turkey
Yemen

Omdurman
Khartoum ★
Wad
Madani

White Nile

Blue Nile

ERITREA Massawa
Asmara ★

YOUR LAND
AND
MY LAND
The Middle
East

We Visit
AFGHANISTAN

Mitchell Lane
PUBLISHERS

Printing   1   2   3   4   5   6   7   8   9

Library of Congress Cataloging-in-Publication Data
Orr, Tamra.
  We visit Afghanistan / by Tamra Orr.
      p. cm. — (Your land and my land—the Middle East)
  Includes bibliographical references and index.
  ISBN 978-1-58415-959-9 (library bound)
  1. Afghanistan—Juvenile literature. I. Title.
  DS351.5.O77 2011
  958.1—dc22
                                                           2011000723
eBook ISBN: 9781612281025

PUBLISHER'S NOTE: This story is based on the author's extensive research, which she believes to be accurate. Documentation of this research is on page 60.

    The Internet sites referenced herein were active as of the publication date. Due to the fleeting nature of some web sites, we cannot guarantee they will all be active when you are reading this book.

    To reflect current usage, we have chosen to use the secular era designations BCE ("before the common era") and CE ("of the common era") instead of the traditional designations BC ("before Christ") and AD (anno Domini, "in the year of the Lord").

Contents

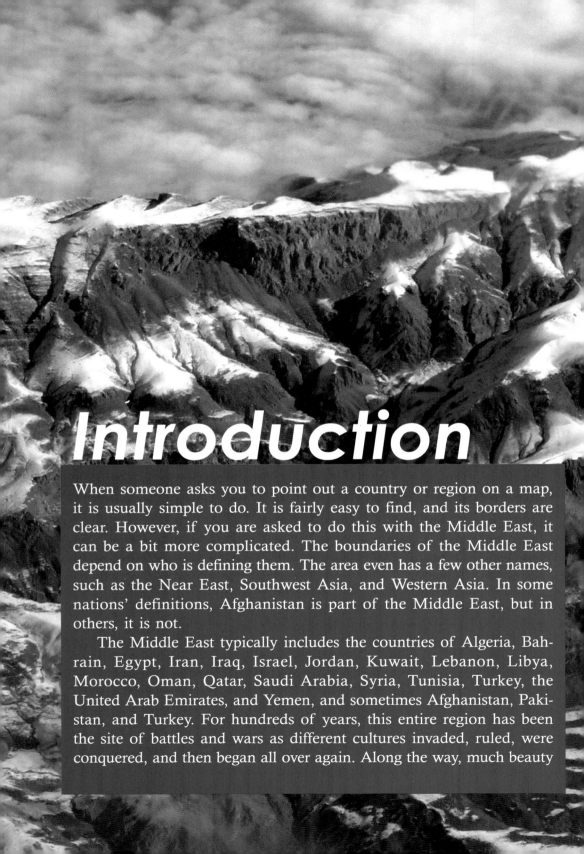

Introduction

When someone asks you to point out a country or region on a map, it is usually simple to do. It is fairly easy to find, and its borders are clear. However, if you are asked to do this with the Middle East, it can be a bit more complicated. The boundaries of the Middle East depend on who is defining them. The area even has a few other names, such as the Near East, Southwest Asia, and Western Asia. In some nations' definitions, Afghanistan is part of the Middle East, but in others, it is not.

The Middle East typically includes the countries of Algeria, Bahrain, Egypt, Iran, Iraq, Israel, Jordan, Kuwait, Lebanon, Libya, Morocco, Oman, Qatar, Saudi Arabia, Syria, Tunisia, Turkey, the United Arab Emirates, and Yemen, and sometimes Afghanistan, Pakistan, and Turkey. For hundreds of years, this entire region has been the site of battles and wars as different cultures invaded, ruled, were conquered, and then began all over again. Along the way, much beauty

in the land was ruined or lost, leaving behind only rubble, memories, and folk tales. Despite this devastation, this land is still full of families who work and laugh and find joy in their lives.

The capital city of Kabul is in the eastern foothills of the Hindu Kush. It is one of the country's oldest cities, thought to have been established between 2000 and 1500 BCE. By 2011, about 3.5 million people were living there.[1]

Welcome to Afghanistan

Many people recognize Afghanistan as a place of war, but it is much more than that. Indeed, different groups of people have fought over this country for centuries. Afghanistan is the buffer between four vastly different cultures: the Islamic Middle East, of which it is part; Central Asia, which includes the former Soviet Union; the Far East (China); and Pakistan. As these people have sought to spread their culture, they have tried to take over Afghanistan. Some were more successful than others.

Although Afghanistan has a great deal of hot, sandy deserts, it also has green, fertile valleys.[2] Because of its extreme weather and spreading deserts, it does not have the variety of wildlife enjoyed by some parts of the world, but it is home to some rare species, such as the snow leopard[3] and the large-billed reed warbler.[4] Migrating birds often stop there to rest, and flying squirrels glide from one tree to the next.[5] Precious gems are found in many of the country's most sacred buildings.

Let's explore the wonders of this Middle Eastern land.

Large-billed reed warbler

WHERE IN THE WORLD IS AFGHANISTAN?

Where in the World

Afghanistan

——————	International boundary
— · — · —	Province (velāyat) boundary
★	National capital
⊙	Province (velāyat) capital
+—+—+	Railroad
————	Road

The existence of two new provinces of Nurestan and Khowst has not been confirmed.

0   100   200 Kilometers

0   100   200 Mil

Lambert Conformal Conic Projection, SP 29 N / 39 N

AFGHANISTAN FACTS AT A GLANCE

Full name: Islamic Republic of Afghanistan

Official languages: Afghan Persian or Dari; Pashto

Population: 29,835,394 (July 2011 estimate)

Land area: 251,827 square miles (652,230 square kilometers); slightly smaller than Texas

Capital: Kabul

Government: Islamic republic

Ethnic makeup: Pashtun 42%, Tajik 27%, Hazara 9%, Uzbek 9%, Turkmen 3%, Baloch 2%, other 4%

Religions: Sunni Muslim 80%, Shia Muslim 19%, other 1%

Exports: Opium, fruits and nuts, handwoven carpets, wool, cotton, hides and pelts, precious and semiprecious gems

Imports: Machinery and other capital goods, food, textiles, petroleum products

Crops: Opium, wheat, fruits and nuts, wool, mutton, sheepskins and lambskins

Average temperatures: August 91°F (33°C); January 19°F (–7°C)

Average rainfall: 12.4 inches (316 millimeters) per year

Highest point: Noshak—24,550 feet (7,485 meters)

Lowest point: Amu Darya—846 feet (258 meters)

Longest river: Amu Darya—1,578 miles (2,540 kilometers); only 600 miles of it is in Afghanistan, where it forms the border with Tajikistan

Flag: The flag was adopted in 1919. During the twentieth century, it went through more design changes than any other flag in the world. The current one has three equal bands running up and down in black, red, and green. Black stands for the past, red for the blood shed in order to gain independence, and green for hope for the future and Islam. The national emblem, in the center, features a mosque with the numbers for the solar year 1298 underneath it. That stands for 1919, the year the country gained  its independence from the United Kingdom of Great Britain and Ireland. There are sheaves of wheat on the left and right with rays from the rising sun. The Muslim creed, "None has the right to be worshiped but Allah, and Muhammad is the Messenger of Allah," and "God is great" are featured.

Source: CIA *World Factbook:* "Afghanistan"

Connecting Afghanistan to Pakistan, the Khyber Pass is considered one of the most important mountain passes of all. It is 33 miles (53 kilometers) long and is made up of two roads. One is for cars, trucks, and buses. The other is for people traveling by foot or camel. The Salang Pass connects south and north Afghanistan. The Wakhjir Pass connects northeast Afghanistan to China.

Into Afghanistan

The band of weary travelers gazed up at the towering mountain before them. The top of it seemed to stretch on forever. It was hard to get solid footing on the bare slopes, dotted only with small bushes and stunted trees, and the men had already been climbing for what felt like days. Their caravans of goods lumbered after them.

One of the men pointed straight ahead and then ran over to look at something. The rest of the men followed. What had he found? Worry turned to relief as they spotted a welcome treasure. On the wall were detailed carvings that showed them which way to go to find the mountain pass. No longer would these travelers have to climb straight up. There was a route through the mountain, and although the journey would still be long, it would not be as long.

For countless years, refugees, armies, explorers, and traders have crossed into and out of Afghanistan over one of the country's many mountain passes, or *kotal*. In a place where half the land is covered in peaks more than 6,000 feet (1,830 meters) high—some soaring up to more than 23,000 feet (7,000 meters)—mountain passes make impossible routes possible, reducing a trip from weeks to days. Drawings, or petroglyphs, on the entrances to mountain passes have helped point people in the right direction. Over time, tunnels have replaced a few of these passes to help make it easier for military troops, battle equipment, and emergency relief workers to enter Afghanistan. These tunnels have reduced travel time from days to hours.

Under the Roof of the World

Afghanistan is bordered by Turkmenistan, Uzbekistan, and Tajikistan in the north; Pakistan in the south and east; Iran in the west; and in the northwest, at the end of the long, skinny Wakhan Corridor, China. Shaped like a leaf, Afghanistan is about the size of Texas. Mountain ranges cross a good part of it, and most of the peaks are so high that some Afghans call them "the roof of the world."

In the northern part of the country are gentle rolling plains. The soil is fertile there and perfect for growing crops such as rice and cotton. Cattle graze, along with sheep and goats. Since only 12 percent of the country's land is able to support crops and animals, this area is highly valued.[1]

The central part of the country is the highlands, with the Hindu Kush ("Mountains of India") looming over the region. Most of the people of Afghanistan live in this area, many of them in small clusters of homes. Each grouping is called a *qal'ah.*

The lowlands of the country are in the southwest. This land of extremes includes fertile soil for growing wheat, barley, and corn, and shallow lakes that host geese, ducks, and swans. It also features the huge Dasht-i-Margo, or "Desert of Death."

Afghanistan is landlocked—it has no coastal borders—but it does have a series of rivers. The largest ones sometimes spill over their banks to create shallow marshes and ponds, but these do not last long. Under the hot summer sun, as well as during frequent periods of drought, many of these bodies of water dry up completely.

Temperature Extremes

Like hot weather? Afghanistan has it. Like cold weather? Just wait for a while. Some of the world's most extreme weather can be in this country. In the summers, much of the country is extremely hot and dry. It is not uncommon for temperatures to go far above 100°F (38°C). Winters bring enough blowing snow to block passes and shut down all travel, and spring can bring flooding as the mountain snows melt.

The Minaret of Jam

Soaring up more than 210 feet (65 meters) into the sky in central Afghanistan is the Minaret of Jam. Minarets are tall, narrow towers that are usually part of a mosque. How they are used depends on whom you ask. Some will say these towers provided the best place for calling people to prayer. Others say they were built to cool the mosque, as they act like an airshaft for pulling in cold air. Still others believe minarets were built simply to let people get higher and thus closer to God.

The Minaret of Jam is the second-tallest brick minaret in the world and is made entirely of baked bricks. The whole tower is covered in intricate and elegant writing and patterns, some of which tell stories from the Koran. Inside are twisting staircases that lead to upper balconies. The tower has stood in Jam, a remote area of Afghanistan, for more than 800 years.

The Blue Mosque in Mazar-e-Sharif

Mazar-e-Sharif in northwest Afghanistan is home to one of the most amazing mosques in the Islamic world. It is said to be the tomb of Hazrat Ali, the son-in-law of the Prophet Muhammad. Every square inch of the mosque is covered in intricate, detailed, and colorful tiles and patterns. Many Muslims come to this mosque to worship, while other visitors come to admire the beauty of its intense colors and design. The area is also known for its white pigeons. Legend states that because the site holds a sacred tomb, all the hundreds of pigeons that fly there turn white within 40 days. Although this is most likely a folk tale, the pigeons at the mosque are indeed all white![2]

Life on the Land

With such extreme temperature differences, few trees, and limited water, it is not too surprising that most creatures have a hard time surviving in Afghanistan. A number of the country's species are in danger, either from being hunted for food or killed for threatening herds. Some of the species at risk include the Asiatic black bear, the Kashmir cave bat, the snow leopard, and the Asiatic cheetah.

The animals that live here are some of the most unusual in the world. The Markhor goat, for example, lives in the mountains of northern Afghanistan. Although its name means "snake eating," it eats nothing other than leaves and grass. It spends twelve hours a day

Although there once were quite a few beautiful sites scattered throughout Afghanistan, many of them have been partly or even completely destroyed over the years by wars, invasions, and Taliban uprisings. For example, some huge Buddha statues were once carved into the side of sandstone cliffs in the Bamyan (also spelled Bamiyan) Valley. They dated all the way back to the second century CE. In 2001, the Taliban destroyed them. They believed the statues were idols, which are contrary to Islamic law.[3]

If you love water, you are sure to find unending beauty in Band-e-Amir, a site of six natural lakes. With water turned bright blue by the carbon dioxide seeping through underground cracks, these lakes sparkle a bright, clear blue in sunshine that is almost blinding. It is little surprise that these lakes are sometimes compared to precious jewels. They are part of the country's first national park, and tourists from all over come to admire them. Along with human visitors, different types of wildlife also stop by, including wolves, foxes, and many different species of birds. Locals fish for carp here, but visitors are limited in an effort to preserve the lake.

One of the most beautiful areas in all of Afghanistan is the Panjshir Valley. Located about 60 miles (100 kilometers) from the capital in the north-central part of the country, it is home to 300,000 people, including those from the ethnic group the Tajiks. Its name means "Five Lions," referring to a legend that five brothers once lived there and built a dam. Besides having groves of walnut trees, fields of wheat, and rivers full of fish, the area is known for emerald and silver mining.

searching for enough food to stay alive. The goat was given its name for its amazing horns. They grow in a corkscrew shape and can reach more than five feet (1.5 meters) long. Unfortunately, those horns are so unique that the species has been hunted almost to extinction. Some hunters take home the horns as trophies, some sell them on the underground (illegal) market, and others grind them into a powder that is used in medical potions.

Other fascinating creatures that call Afghanistan home are the rhesus macaque, the Alpine musk deer, the giant red flying squirrel, and the Karakul sheep. The rhesus macaque lives in very large and extremely noisy groups. It climbs and swims well but spends most of its time on the ground.

The Alpine musk deer is unusual because the males do not have antlers. Instead, they have two upper teeth that grow like small tusks. Males also have a gland on their belly that produces a smell used in perfumes all over the world. So many of these deer have been killed for that gland that their numbers are also at risk.

The giant red flying squirrel does not actually fly, but compared to most other squirrel species, it could be considered a giant. It is commonly 15 inches (38 centimeters) long, one of the largest squirrels in the world. Instead of flying, it spreads its arms and legs wide, and the skin between its limbs stretches out like wings. This allows the squirrel to glide up to 250 feet (75 meters) at a time.

Karakul sheep are tough animals that survive in the Afghan heat. They store extra fat in their tail, much like camels do in their humps. They can use this fat during long periods of drought. Their wool is used for spinning into yarn for carpets and blankets.

Migrating birds often take a much-needed break in Afghanistan. The Siberian red crane stops to rest while traveling from summering in Russia to wintering in India. Flamingos used to come by, but after years of drought, their rest spots have dried up too much to use.

Markhor goat

In 2009, an international team of archaeologists discovered some of the oldest oil paintings in the world inside the caves of Afghanistan's Bamyan Valley. Almost 50 of the many caves had murals painted on the rock walls. They showed images of Buddha and his followers, and experts believe they date all the way back to the mid-600s CE.[1]

A Trip Back Through Time

Imagine for a moment that you have somehow been transported through time to the Afghanistan of 7000 BCE. What would you see when you looked around? Chances are, unless you happened to start in one of the large cities, the landscape would be very similar to that of today's Afghanistan. Unlike many other countries, Afghanistan has changed very little with the passing of the centuries.

People have been living in this area of the world for thousands of years. In fact, the Middle East is sometimes referred to as "the cradle of civilization." Many of the people who moved into this region were farmers who struggled to grow crops and raise animals in the limited fertile land. They continue to do so today.

Although Afghanistan is hot, dry, and difficult to live in, surrounding cultures that wanted to put this crossroads of Asia under their control repeatedly invaded the land. A look at the country's history shows a cycle of invasions, victories, losses, and new invasions. Each culture brought violence and revolution, but it also brought arts, language, technology, and traditions that have made Afghanistan a diverse and unusual country.

Ancient Afghanistan

The first people to come to the land now known as Afghanistan were from central Asia. They settled in the area and, over the next one thousand years, divided the country into three sections. By the sixth century BCE, the country had become a part of the Persian Empire.

That lasted until Alexander the Great from the land of Macedonia came along. Around 330 BCE, he captured Kabul and then kept going, claiming most of the country for Greece until his death some years later. His people greatly influenced the growing culture, including adding an alphabet and a government system.

During the first century CE, Afghanistan became part of the Kushan Empire, and it was not long before the country was the center of the religion called Buddhism. Buddhist monks built monasteries in cliffs, digging out the soil and rocks to create rooms, halls, and chambers. Huge, towering statues of Buddha were carved into the sides of limestone mountains. These are the statues of Bamyan Valley.

Several hundred years after Buddhism arrived, the Huns came from the north and took over the country. Their control lasted for three centuries; and then, in 642, the Arab Empire took control. Buddhism was pushed aside in favor of a different religion known as Islam. This religion would be a part of Afghanistan's daily life from that point forward.

From One Victor to the Next
Afghanistan continued to change hands over the centuries. It belonged to Asia until the tenth century, and then went to Mahmud of Ghazni. He is considered one of the greatest rulers the country ever had. After Mahmud's death, Afghanistan was taken over by the Turks. The next invasion came when Genghis Khan and his Mongols arrived. These hostile people took control through violence in 1219, tearing through the country's biggest cities and killing more than a million people in a matter of days.

After Genghis Khan died, one of his descendants, a man named Babur, took control. He remained in the land, making it part of the Mughal Empire, until he finally decided to move on to India and see how much he could conquer there. For the next two centuries, Afghanistan was split. Part of it was under the rule of the Mughals, while the other was under the rule of a group from Persia called the Safavids.

In 1747, a group of Afghans called the Loya Jirga, or "grand council," met for nine days. They came to the conclusion that their

Bagh-e Babur. Babur died at the age of 47. He was first buried in a mausoleum in the capital city of Agra. Roughly nine years later, he was buried in the beautiful garden Bagh-e Babur in Kabul, now in Afghanistan. The inscription on his tomb reads (in Persian): "If there is a paradise on earth, it is this, it is this, it is this!"

country should be united. Led by their king, Ahmad Shah Durrani, they created an army and then marched out to conquer the northern and western parts to bring them together.

The Wars Continue

During the 1830s, Great Britain invaded India and took over. The British were concerned that Russia would try to take the territory away from them. When they heard a rumor that Russia was planning to invade Afghanistan, they were more concerned. In what was sometimes called the Great Game, they sent their own troops into Afghanistan to strengthen the borders.

In 1839, the First Anglo-Afghan War began when 21,000 British and Indian troops invaded Afghanistan. It lasted until 1842, when Britain withdrew. Thousands were killed or injured.

Ahmad Shah Durrani was the founder of the Durrani Empire and is regarded by many to be responsible for creating the modern state of Afghanistan.

A little less than 40 years later, in 1878, the Second Anglo-Afghan War began. Once again, the British invaded Afghanistan. Although the British technically won, they were not able to control the people, who were angry about British rule. The British tried a third time to take over the country in 1919, but this time, instead of withdrawing, the Brits clearly lost, and Afghanistan became independent. August 19 is now Afghanistan's official Independence Day.

After Independence

Life in Afghanistan began to change dramatically after it gained its independence. From 1933 to 1973, it was ruled by Mohammad Zahir.

The First Anglo-Afghan War was fought by men known as the Khalsa, or brotherhood of "warrior saints." They were considered one of the most powerful armies in the world at the time, and between their mercenary training and their weaponry, they were a mighty enemy.

This king created a close friendship with the Soviet Union. Its government, in Moscow, provided a great deal of money to the country, helping to build roads and an army. However, in 1979, the Soviets invaded and installed their own man as president of Afghanistan.

Not surprisingly, the Afghan people fought back. Rebel groups called mujahideen formed and began to fight a jihad, or holy war, to get the Soviets out of power. The United States joined the fight, and by 1989, the Soviets were leaving Afghanistan.

Unfortunately, life in Afghanistan did not improve after Soviet withdrawal. Instead, a number of different rebel groups sprang up and fought each other for power. A group of Islamic students known as the Taliban emerged the winner. By 1998, the Taliban had not only taken over almost all of the country, it had put harsh and violent laws into place that went against basic human rights. The Taliban government changed Afghanistan and brought war back to daily life. When the Taliban helped protect Osama bin Laden, a terrorist leader, the United States responded with missiles and demands for Bin Laden, which were ignored. A few years later, Bin Laden engineered the September 11, 2001, attacks on the U.S. World Trade Center and the Pentagon. The War on Terror had begun, and Afghanistan was right in the middle of it.

Afghanistan Today

Since 2001, when thousands of troops from a variety of countries around the world marched into Afghanistan, many changes have taken place. In 2004, the people were allowed to vote for the president of their country for the first time in decades, and a new constitution was put into place. Elected officials would serve for five years, and the National Assembly would make the laws. This group includes the Wolesi Jirga (House of the People) and the Meshrano Jirga (House of the Elders). A number of those representatives are women—a huge change in this land.

For hundreds of years, the leaders of Afghanistan depended on the Loya Jirga, or grand council, to make the biggest and most important decisions for the country. This style of governing was based on an ancient tradition that began with the nomads from Central Asia. They would gather inside a tent in the middle of the desert and talk until they were able to elect a new leader.

Today, Afghanistan is divided into 34 different sections known as provinces. These are further divided into almost 400 separate districts. Although the current style of government has a governor for each province, most Afghans do not follow the governor's decisions. Instead, as their ancestors did before them, they listen to and follow the decrees of the local *shura,* or council, and *jirga,* or tribal assembly.

In 2005, the United Nations made an agreement with Afghanistan that outlined a five-year plan for rebuilding the country. Meanwhile, the Taliban has continued to fight for control of the government, battling the U.S. military, the Afghan National Army, and people from

IRAN
Ahvāz
āsirīyah
Abādān
Kermān

A Trip Back Through Time

3

In 2010, a *shura* met with leaders from the British military to discuss how to move Taliban fighters away from populated areas of the southern Nad-e-Ali district. The plan also involved setting up new patrol bases in the region.

the United Nations. In 2009, U.S. President Barack Obama sent additional troops to Afghanistan to keep fighting this dangerous rebel group.

Although some experts have stated that U.S. troops would be sent home and the country returned to its people by the year 2014, some people doubted it would ever happen. Even after Osama bin Laden was killed in May 2011, the Taliban remained strong, determined, and violent.

Afghanistan is known for its gems, including the bright blue lapis lazuli. An Afghani man examines each one to find just the right piece. The stone is turned into beautiful jewelry, and it is often used in ceramics, tiles, statues, and even buildings.

Creating a Desert Home

For days, the men had trudged across the land. First, they moved quickly, riding comfortably in automobiles, but as the path became rockier and steeper, they had to switch to riding horses. Now, after an entire day in the saddle, they were almost falling asleep through sheer exhaustion. The Sar-e Sang mines they had heard so many stories about still seemed a million miles away. Before they got there, they would most likely have to endure the threats of wild hogs, hungry wolves, and snow-filled mountain passes. Why must treasure be hidden in such desolation?

The strength to keep moving came from picturing their ultimate goal: the glitter of intense blue stone embedded within the mines, the coveted lapis lazuli. This stone's vibrant color had been used throughout Afghanistan in mosques and other holy places. It was in tiles, dishes, and ancient tombs, and even in the jewelry of the wealthy. The stone was a ticket to fortune—if the men could find enough and then mine it without breaking it.

The Sar-e Sang mines were nothing new to the Afghan people. The mines had been providing the opaque lapis lazuli for thousands of years. Stones were traded with merchants from Europe, Asia, and Africa, who made beads with it or used its powder to tinge eye makeup.

For hundreds of years, the method of fire-set mining was rough at best. Fires were started at the sites of the stones, and once the tunnels were hot, the fire was doused and cold water was thrown on the rocks.

The sudden cooling caused the rocks to crack and, with luck, to expose the precious stones. Too often this method also cracked the treasure the miners were trying to reach. As firewood became more and more scarce, however, this method faded away. With it, mining lapis lazuli also faded, as the stone became too hard to reach, find, and extract.[1]

Back to the Land

Although many people in Afghanistan have spent their lives searching for lapis lazuli, as well as for some of the emeralds and rubies scattered across the country, the majority of people are simply farmers. They work very hard, often able to grow and harvest barely enough to feed

Between frequent droughts and rising food prices, it has become more difficult for Afghans to grow wheat. The farmers have had to rely on wheat seed imported from other countries in order to keep their families fed.

FYI FACT:

One of the few types of trees that grow well in Afghanistan is the date palm. It is able to survive because it has very long roots that grow far enough down into the ground to reach the few water reserves in this arid land. The average female tree produces 100 pounds (45 kilograms) or more of fruit each year, and many people depend on it to survive.[2]

Goat farmers in Afghanistan keep busy taking care of their animals. Some of the goats in this country produce a fiber called cashmere, which is exceptionally soft and is used to make many different kinds of luxury clothing. Cashmere is actually the undercoat of goats, which protects them from cold weather.

their own families. The main crops they grow are wheat, corn, barley, rice, nuts, and fruits such as melons and grapes. Almost all of it is raised without the modern conveniences of machines, fertilizers, and pesticides. Some farmers also keep herds of sheep and goats, which they raise for their milk, meat, and wool.

People like Malalai Joya bring courage and hope to the people of Afghanistan. Joya has spoken out against the way her country treats women, and in doing so has faced death threats and harassment within her homeland.

Chapter 5

Afghan People to Know

Like many other countries, Afghanistan is full of heroes, artists, and other talented and famous people. Let's meet a few of them.

Bashir Bakhtiari (unknown birth date–)
Writer, artist, and filmmaker Bashir Bakhtiari, who uses his pen name Baache Azra, is known throughout Afghanistan for both his written words and his thought-provoking cartoons. Bakhtiari has drawn logos, posters, billboards, and book covers, and his comics have been published on the Internet. In addition, he has made over 200 documentaries and television commercials. Although his drawings are popular with many, they have also gotten him in trouble. Under the Taliban rule in Afghanistan, people who speak out against the government may be beaten by police, imprisoned, or even executed. For his safety, Bakhtiari left Afghanistan and moved to New Zealand.

Sharbat Gula (1972–)
For many years the cover photos on *National Geographic* magazine have captured the attention of millions of readers. In June 1985, a beautiful Afghan girl with startlingly bright eyes was featured on the cover of the magazine. She was a refugee living in a Pakistan camp when the Soviets occupied Afghanistan. Although her identity was

unknown, her image became the symbol of the battle raging in the land. Her face is still considered one of the most recognized photographs in the world. In 2002, *National Geographic* returned to Afghanistan to track down the woman and to get her name. By then Gula was thirty and a wife and mother, but she had never seen the famous picture of her. Her photo was taken again and featured in the magazine, and she was the subject of a television documentary called *Search for the Afghan Girl.*[1]

Malalai Joya (1978–)

Some international news companies have called Malalai Joya either the most famous or the bravest woman in all of Afghanistan. Not only has she taken a stand against the Taliban and other war criminals in her country, she has spoken publicly about them in a place that does not easily accept outspoken women. Voted to the Afghan parliament in 2005, she was suspended for insulting other parliament members. She is fighting to get her place back and has the support of many well-known and powerful people in multiple countries. In 2010, *Time* magazine named Joya one of the 100 most influential people in the world for her battles to protect human rights. Her autobiography, *A Woman Among Warlords: The Extraordinary Story of an Afghan Who Dared to Raise Her Voice,* was published in 2009.

Meena Keshwar Kamal (1956–1987)

One of Afghanistan's other outspoken women was Meena Keshwar Kamal. She once said, "Afghan women are like sleeping lions, when awoken, they can play a wonderful role in any social revolution." Kamal was the founder of RAWA, the Revolutionary Association of the Women of Afghanistan. She fought hard to get equal rights, as well as education, for women in her country. Although she was assassinated when she was only thirty, RAWA continues to operate, secretly running orphanages and schools for girls.[2]

Abdul Ahad Mohmand (1959–)

Abdul Ahad Mohmand was the first Afghan pilot to travel into space. After serving in the Afghan Air Force, Mohmand trained in the Soviet Union for possible space travel. In 1988, he flew on the Soviet spacecraft Soyuz TM-6 and spent nine days aboard the Mir Space Station. That same year, he was named the Hero of the Soviet Union for his hard work and dedication.

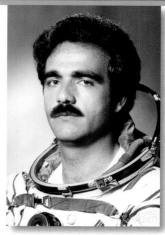

Nekqadama (1979–)

In 2010, Nekqadama was introduced to the world through an article that profiled her unusual life. Born in Afghanistan, she and her family left while she was still a baby and went to Pakistan. They lived in a refugee camp until she married a cousin who lived in the United States. After divorcing, she discovered that the military needed translators, and soon she was on the way to Camp Leatherneck, a U.S. Marine base in Helmand, Afghanistan—bulletproof vest and all. Although she is a U.S. soldier, many of the people relate to her as a fellow Afghan.

Ahmad Zahir (1946–1979)

Sometimes referred to as the Afghan version of Elvis Presley, Zahir was a very popular musician throughout Afghanistan. He played the mandolin and accordion, sang, and wrote his own songs. He began playing music in high school, and by the 1970s, he was learning from some of the best Afghan musicians. He recorded more than 19 albums and became a national hero. When the government in Afghanistan changed in the 1970s, Zahir wrote songs with lyrics that stirred political controversy. He was assassinated for his outspokenness in 1979 at the age of thirty-three.

The age-old tradition of calling Muslims to prayer is shown in this 1879 painting by Jean-Léon Gérôme, *A Muezzin Calling from the Top of a Minaret the Faithful to Prayer*. This tradition is carried on in parts of Afghanistan, although machines have replaced some of the muezzins.

Chapter 6

The Word of Islam

The silence of the dawn was broken by the beloved sound of the muezzin's voice as it echoed throughout the city. His words spoke to the faithful of Islam, asking them from the top of the mosque to come to prayer. Five times every day, the holy man's voice is heard. He calls out at sunrise and again at midday, in midafternoon, at sunset, and finally at the fall of night. Each time, the followers of Islam, called Muslims, stop what they are doing and, in a very formal and careful process, kneel and pray. First they cleanse themselves by washing their hands, mouth, face, arms, neck, ears, and feet several times with water.[1] Next, they turn toward Mecca, the birthplace of their prophet, Muhammad. They face the Kaabah, a cube-shaped building that is often covered with a black cloth. With set gestures and movements, the people pray to Allah. In the past, the muezzin was a talented holy man. While there are still some muezzin, the call may now come from a recording sent out over powerful speakers.

Even when the muezzin is not calling people to prayer, the basic beliefs of Islam are present in Afghanistan. The religion guides what people do, wear, eat, think, and say. It determines their government's decisions, their attitudes about the world, and their morals about how life should be lived.

The Muslims of Afghanistan

Almost all of the people living in Afghanistan are Muslim. In fact, it is against the law for citizens to follow any other religion. Islam is a

39

type of faith that focuses on creating laws that are thought to have been designed and decreed by God. Unlike in the United States and many other countries, there is no separation between church and state.

The basic philosophy of Islam is called the *shahadah*. This is a statement, or creed, that says, "There is no god but God (Allah) and Muhammad is His Prophet (Messenger)." The religion has five pillars, or basic beliefs, that the people follow:

1) *Reciting the creed.* The *shahadah* is spoken at each prayer session.
2) *Attending daily prayer.* Followers must pray dutifully and perfectly at five set times each day.
3) *Giving money to the poor.* A portion of the money each Muslim earns must be given to those in need.
4) *Making a pilgrimage to Mecca.* Every faithful Muslim is to take a journey (Hajj) to Mecca at least once in his or her lifetime.

The Kaabah is inside the Masjid al-Haram, the Sacred Mosque, in Mecca, Saudi Arabia. Praying is a group activity in the Muslim tradition. Every phrase, movement, and gesture is taught to children from a very early age.

Islam has two main branches of belief. The Sunnis believe that anyone who has learned the ways of Islam may become a leader. The Shi'ites, on the other hand, believe that only descendants of the Prophet Muhammad are eligible to be true religious leaders. The differences do not end there, however. Sunnis lower their heads to mats during prayer, and believe that Allah has a body that can be seen sometimes as he directly controls humans' actions and lives. The Shi'ites lower their heads to hard clay during prayer. They believe that Allah cannot be seen, and while he knows all, he does not influence how people act.

(5) *Fasting during Ramadan.* During the month of Ramadan, Muslims are not to eat or drink from sunrise to sunset. Some people, such as pregnant women, are exempt from this rule.

Religion plays such a large role in Afghanistan that in many ways it has united the country—but it has also created some serious problems. The faith has allowed quite a few of the men in this culture to treat women as inferior people. Many men believe that because of the religious rules of modesty, they have the right to control and punish women for such actions as showing their faces in public. A number of the stories about the treatment of Afghan women have been on international news.

While most Muslims are peaceful people and do not believe in violence, some Muslim groups have turned to terrorism to spread their faith. Members of the Taliban, for example, believe so strongly in their interpretation of Islam that they advocate killing anyone who does not adopt the religion. This group has destroyed many relics throughout Afghanistan, believing that these items are blasphemous, and it has been behind some extremely violent actions against people around the world. Believing that many of the favorite hobbies of the Afghan people do not honor the principles of Islam, the Taliban put an end to many types of entertainment. While the Taliban was in power, sports stadiums were used for executing people instead of playing games. Kite flying was banned, as were hobbies such as bird watching and even watching television. The Taliban also helped bring war with the United States to their country by harboring Osama bin Laden, and the changes the war brought will be felt for generations to come.

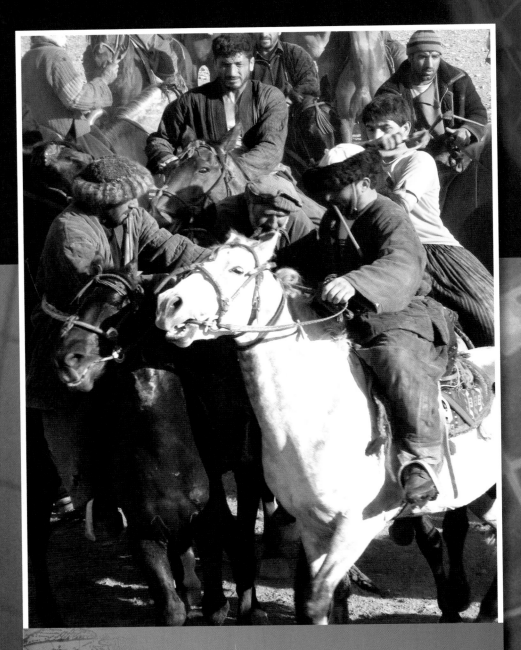

One of the most popular games in Afghanistan is also a violent and dangerous one that calls for as much bravery as it does skill. Welcome to the game of goat grabbing!

Goat Grabbing and Kite Fighting

The *chapandaz* hit the ground with a thud, knocking the air out of his lungs. He was grateful for his high leather boots and padded jacket because they helped keep his injuries to simple bruises instead of broken bones. His horse waited patiently next to him while he grabbed his wolf-skin cap and whip from the ground and then swung himself into the saddle. In seconds, this player was back in the game.

Buzkashi, or goat grabbing, is the national sport of Afghanistan. It is played in many places, from big-city stadiums to open lots, and is often the entertainment of choice at weddings and other celebrations. The players, called *chapandaz,* are all men. Women are not only banned from playing the game, but in some parts of the country, they may not even watch it. It is a rough sport that often results in a number of injuries and sometimes in death. In the game, two teams compete for possession of the headless carcass of a calf or goat. They must drop the body in a scoring area that is almost impossible to reach, since multiple players block it with their horses, whips, and even knives. It takes years of training for players to become skilled at the game. Most of them are well over forty years old. It also takes five years for the horses to be properly trained. They have to be taught to stand still and wait when a player falls off or is grabbing the calf, and then, as soon as the rider is back on top, take off and return to the fray. Winners of the *buzkashi* are often given gifts, such as money, clothes, or new turbans.[1]

Wicked and Windy

When you think of flying a kite, you may think of simply having fun on a windy day. Chances are, if you lived in Afghanistan and you thought about flying a kite, you would be gearing up for battle in a fierce competition. The art of kite fighting, or *gudiparan bazi,* is well known in this country. For hundreds of years, people have enjoyed sending a kite up into the sky and watching it fight with other kites. When the Taliban was in power, kite flying was illegal, but people still flew them secretly.

An Afghan man prepares his kite for the contest.

Kite fighting takes the teamwork of two people. One, the *charka gir,* holds a spool of wire and lets it out or takes it in. The *gudiparan baz,* on the other hand, is in charge of where the kite flies and how it moves.

The kites used in this kind of contest come in all different sizes. Some are only about a foot in diameter, while others are as large as six feet. All of them are made of thin paper and bamboo. Instead of using string on the kite, however, Afghan players use wire coated in glue made of rice, water, and ground glass. When the kites take to the air, each team battles to see whose wire will slice through the wire of another team. Sometimes the battle is over in seconds and sometimes it takes as long as a half hour or more. It depends a great deal on how much wind there is and how skilled the players are. When a team's wire is cut, the kite drifts off into the sky and may be found miles away. Whoever finds it is free to keep it and use it.

Other Games

Other than grabbing goats and flying kites, Afghans enjoy several other sports. Wrestling or *pehlwani* is popular, as is *gursai,* a game that is as much fun to watch as it is to play. In *gursai,* the players hold their left foot with their right hand and then hop around trying to knock others down without falling themselves. Children often enjoy *buzul-bazi,* a game that is much like marbles only it uses sheep knucklebones for rolling instead. Soccer is also popular.

Afghan boys playing soccer

Meals in Afghanistan often have as much religious importance as nutritional value. Most meals are eaten while sitting on the ground and in communal settings. Men may break their day's fast with a simple meal of fruit and dates.

Family Time

In Afghanistan, hospitality is very important and part of the code of honor. Guests stopping by at mealtime are traditionally given the very best food the host has to offer, even if it means the rest of the family members will go hungry.

Mealtime in an Afghan home is quite different than it is in some other countries. For example, meals are eaten while sitting on the floor on colorful cushions called *toshak*. Under these cushions are colorful carpets. Dishes are placed on mats on the carpets. During the hot summer months, meals might be served outside under the cooling shade of a tree. During the winter, however, everyone eats inside, sitting around a blanket-covered low table, or *sandali*. To keep warm, the blanket is placed over everyone's legs. A *mangal,* or small charcoal oven, is placed under the table to provide heat.

The Afghans do not use cutlery to eat their food. Instead, they use their right hands (never the left). Large platters full of food are passed around, and people scoop a serving onto their plate. Before each course, a bowl and jug, or *haftawa-wa-lagan,* are passed around so that hands can be washed.

Quabili palau

On the Menu
Some of the most common foods served in Afghanistan include a dish called *palau,* or rice with fruit and some kind of meat, usually mutton or

lamb. Often this is accompanied by a type of plain flat bread called *naan* that is used to scoop up the rest of the food. Yogurt or *mast* is a common side dish. Chickpeas are popular, especially in a dish called hummus, and eggplant is served in many different forms. Kebabs, another favorite dish, are made by grilling bite-sized pieces of meat and vegetables on long sticks.

Because silverware is not used, long pieces of thick bread or naan like these are often broken into pieces and used to scoop up bites of food. These are utensils you can eat!

Meet the Family

Afghan families are close, and several generations may live in one home. It is not unusual for cousins and other single relatives to share the same house as well. As people get older, they are traditionally given more respect. In Afghanistan, the men are definitely the head of the family, and they are allowed to have more than one wife. In this culture, men are the ones in power. They have strong rules about how women are allowed to dress and behave. At the same time, women are largely in charge of what happens within the household. They make sure that food is pre-pared and that children are tended to carefully. Couples are eager to have children, and boys are extra welcome. Divorce is rare—it is strongly discouraged and rarely granted, and the husband must agree to it. Wives who seek a divorce are often ostracized (disowned by their family), and they lose economic support.[1]

What do the Afghan people wear? Men typically put on baggy cotton pants and a long cotton shirt with a colorful sash around the waist. Clothes are loose to help them keep cool, and are usually white to help reflect the sun's heat. On their head the men wear a skullcap and then a turban. The women, on the other hand, wear a long loose shirt or flowing dress over baggy trousers while at home. A large shawl wraps around their head. If women go out in public, they usually put on a burka (also spelled *burqa*), or long veil, which covers them from head to toe. For some women, this garment is essential to their religion and the rules of their husbands. For others, the burka is not necessary.

Some Afghan men spend most of their days out in the field working on the small amount of land that is fertile. Others search for jobs, which, with an unemployment rate of 35 percent, are difficult to find. The women typically remain in the home, cleaning and cooking. During harvest time, they may join their husbands with the hard work of bringing in the crops. Most children are not enrolled in school. On average, 46 percent of Afghan children between the ages of seven and thirteen, especially girls, do not attend school. Even if they do, they are often in classrooms that do not have enough certified teachers or materials.[2] Many of the children stay home to tend flocks and help

Farming is a difficult and exhausting job that often requires the help of every member of the family. Wives, sons, and daughters all step in to help plant and harvest the crops.

School is primarily geared for boys from wealthy families. The majority of children stay home in order to help their parents in the home and in the field. Reading and writing are not highly valued in this culture.

care for younger brothers and sisters. Because of this lack of formal education, less than 45 percent of boys over the age of 15 can read or write—and less than 15 percent of girls can.[3]

FYI FACT:

The people of Afghanistan put a great deal of effort and skill into making their world a more beautiful place. With needle and thread, they embroider everything from the grain bags they use to carry produce to and from the market to breathtaking carpets recognized all over the world for their patterns and color.

Muslims gather at Kandahar Airfield, Afghanistan, to celebrate the start of Eid al-Adha. The holiday marks the beginning of the hajj, the annual pilgrimage to Mecca.

Time to Celebrate

In Afghanistan, during the ninth month of the Muslim calendar, you might find yourself glancing at the clock more often than usual. As your empty stomach rumbles, you might start checking the skyline for signs that the day is over and the sun is getting ready to set.

During Ramadan, every Muslim proves his or her devotion to Muhammad each day by fasting (not eating or drinking) from sunrise to sunset. The only people who do not follow this ritual are the sick and weak, nursing or pregnant women, soldiers, and very young children. The month may seem long, but when it is over, there is great celebration. It is time for festivals to begin!

Enjoy Eid al-Fitr and Eid al-Adha

When the month of fasting comes to an end, it is time to make up for lost time and feast. The celebration of Eid al-Fitr goes on for three days. Friends and families gather to eat and talk. Children are given new clothes in honor of this special time.

As soon as this holiday ends, Eid al-Adha begins. During this time period, anyone who is planning to make the journey to Mecca starts preparing for the trip. A feast is held, and food is shared with the poor.

Other Holidays

Because almost everyone in the country is Muslim, Afghanistan's holidays center on that faith. Just as most cultures celebrate the beginning of a new year, so does Afghanistan. Called Nowruz, which means

Eating tasty and special treats like the ones laid out in this home is part of the Eid celebration. Many women take pride in preparing delicious recipes for their family and friends.

"new day," the holiday begins on the first day of spring (March 21 or 22). Special desserts are prepared, some of which take days to make.

A number of Muslims feel it is not part of their faith to celebrate individual birthdays. Instead, they celebrate Mawlid-un Nabi, the day their prophet was born and, years later, died. Stories of the Prophet's life, as well as all he accomplished, are told in mosques and homes. Songs are sung in his honor, and many buildings are decorated.

A Country of Opposites
Afghanistan is a country like many others—it is full of beautiful landscapes, fascinating wildlife, and interesting people. Over the years,

June 1 is known as Children's Day throughout Afghanistan, and is organized by the Ministry of Women's Affairs. To celebrate the day, children sing and perform in a play for parents and friends. In return, the children are given school supplies, toys, candy, and clothing.

as invaders have waged wars in order to control the region and extremist groups have battled to gain power, the land and its people have paid a very high price. As the war in the Middle East rages on, there is growing hope that, with time, Afghanistan will recover and return to being a place that people want to visit and families can grow in freedom and safety.

Afghani Hummus

Hummus is one of the most common recipes found throughout the Middle East. It is eaten with all three meals and served in most restaurants. The word *hummus* is Arabic for "chickpea" or "garbanzo bean," the main ingredient in the recipe. You can serve it with carrot sticks and other vegetables, crackers, corn chips, or pita bread for dipping.

Ingredients
1 clove garlic, chopped
1 (15 oz) can chickpeas, drained with
    liquid reserved
2 tablespoons lemon juice
2 teaspoons ground cumin
½ teaspoon salt
1 tablespoon olive oil
Dash cayenne pepper or paprika

Directions
1. Put all of the ingredients except the reserved liquid in a blender.
2. Blend on low speed until you have a smooth paste.
3. Slowly add reserved liquid until the hummus is the thickness you like.
4. Serve with a dash of cayenne pepper or paprika on top.

Afghani Kite

Here are the directions for making a simple kite that might be used for fun in Afghanistan. We do not recommend coating the string with glass for *gudiparan bazi*, however.

You will need
An adult
13-gallon plastic trash bag (white is best)
Scissors
Two wooden dowels or straight sticks (one 24 inches long, the other 20 inches long)
Ruler
Markers
String or fishing line
Clear packing tape
Ribbons

Directions
1. With **an adult's** help, cut open the trash bag so that it forms a flat sheet.
2. Pick up the long stick and measure six inches down from the top. Make a mark. Pick up the short stick and place it at the mark on the long one. Form a cross with the sticks.
3. Tie the sticks together with some string and add packing tape to make the joint stronger.
4. Place the sticks on the trash bag. Using the ruler, draw a line around the frame from the top of one stick to the end of the second stick and then down to the bottom point.
5. With the ruler, continue making the outline on the other side of the cross. Your marks should make a diamond.
6. With the scissors, cut the diamond two inches wider than the one you just drew.
7. Turn the kite over and decorate it with markers.
8. On the undecorated side, lay the sticks on the diamond shape and fold the edges over the stick frame. Tape them down.
9. Cut a piece of string or fishing line about 20 inches (50 centimeters) long. Poke holes on either side of the long stick at the top and bottom of the kite. Thread the string through the holes, going around the stick, at the top and bottom of the kite. Tie the string in a knot. Add some tape to keep the holes from tearing.
10. Tie the rest of the string to the middle of the piece of attached string.
11. Tape ribbon to the bottom of the kite to make its tail.
12. Take the kite outside on a windy day and give it a try.

BCE

Unknown	People arrive from central Asia to settle throughout Afghanistan.
Sixth century	Afghanistan is part of the Persian Empire.
329–336	Alexander the Great takes control of the region.

CE

c. 130	Under Kushan ruler Kanishka, Buddhism begins to flourish in Afghanistan.
300–400	The Buddhas of Bamyan are carved.
642	The country is taken over by the Arab empire, which introduces Islam.
962–1030	The Ghaznavid Dynasty is in power.
c. 1140–1219	The Ghurid Sultanate, from central Afghanistan, is in power.
1219	Genghis Khan and the Mongols arrive in Afghanistan.
c. 1500–1747	Mughal-Safavid Rivalry keeps Afghanistan split.
1747	King Ahmad Shah begins uniting the different parts of Afghanistan.
1839–1842	First Anglo-Afghan War is fought.
1878–1880	Second Anglo-Afghan War is waged.
1919	Afghanistan gains independence.
1933–1973	Afghanistan is ruled by a monarchy.
1973	A military coup by former Prime Minister Mohammed Daoud Khan abolishes the monarchy; Daoud declares himself president.
1975–1977	Daoud presents a new constitution and makes numerous reforms.
1978	Officers loyal to the People's Democratic Party lead a communist countercoup; Daoud is killed.
1979	The Soviets invade Afghanistan.
1989	The Soviets withdraw from Afghanistan.
1996	The Taliban takes Kabul and creates the Islamic Emirate of Afghanistan. Except for Saudi Arabia, Pakistan, and the United Arab Emirates, the world does not recognize the Taliban's Islamic Emirate as the official government of Afghanistan.
1998	The Taliban has almost complete control of Afghanistan.
2001	Al-Qaeda, run by Osama bin Laden, attacks the Pentagon and the World Trade Center in the United States. U.S. President George W. Bush wages the War on Terror in Afghanistan and topples the Taliban.
2004	Hamid Karzai becomes president; a new constitution is introduced.
2009	Karzai is elected to a second term.
2010	In November, NATO leaders gather for a summit in Lisbon, where Afghanistan tops the agenda.
2011	U.S. Navy Seal Team 6 kills Osama bin Laden in Pakistan on May 1. NATO forces continue to clash with the Taliban. U.S. President Barack Obama is set to begin a gradual drawdown of U.S. troops in July.

CHAPTER NOTES

Chapter 1. Afghanistan Overview
1. Afghanistan Culture, "Kabul Afghanistan," 2009, http://www.afghanistan-culture.com/kabul-afghanistan.html
2. CIA—*The World Factbook:* "Afghanistan" https://www.cia.gov/library/publications/the-world-factbook/geos/af.html
3. Andrew Revkin, "Afghanistan Protects 33 Species," Dot Earth, *The New York Times,* June 9, 2009, http://dotearth.blogs.nytimes.com/2009/06/09/afghanistan-protects-33-species/
4. Jennifer Harper, "Rare Bird Discovered in Afghan Mountains," *Washington Times,* January 15, 2010, http://www.washingtontimes.com/news/2010/jan/15/hidden-for-years-in-afghanistan-rare-bird-discover/
5. US AID: Afghanistan, "National Environmental Protection Agency Declares Afghanistan's First Protected Species List," press release, June 3, 2009, http://afghanistan.usaid.gov/en/Article.673.aspx

Chapter 2. Into Afghanistan
1. CIA—*The World Factbook:* "Afghanistan" https://www.cia.gov/library/publications/the-world-factbook/geos/af.html
2. Tales of Asia, "Mazar-e-Sharif" http://www.talesofasia.com/afghanistan-mazar.htm
3. "The Destruction of the Statues in Bamiyan" http://www.photogrammetry.ethz.ch/research/bamiyan/buddha/destruction.html

Chapter 3. A Trip Back Through Time
1. Eti Bonn-Muller, "Oldest Oil Paintings | Bamiyan, Afghanistan," *Archaeology,* Vol. 62, No. 1, January/February 2009, http://www.archaeology.org/0901/topten/oldest_oil_paintings.html

Chapter 4. Creating a Desert Home
1. Dr. Peter Bancroft, *Gem and Crystal Treasures* (Fallbrook, CA: Western Enterprises/Mineralogical Record, 1984), "Lapis Lazuli from Afghanistan" http://www.palagems.com/lapis_lazuli_bancroft.htm
2. Innvista, "Dates," http://www.innvista.com/health/foods/fruits/dates.htm

Chapter 5. Afghan People to Know
1. TV Documentaries: "In Search of the Afghan Girl" http://www.abc.net.au/tv/documentaries/stories/s676998.htm
2. Revolutionary Association of the Women of Afghanistan http://www.rawa.org/index.php

Chapter 6. The Word of Islam
1. Kristheena Irwin, "Ablution—Cleansing of the Body and Spirit," *Suite 101.com,* July 20, 2009, http://www.suite101.com/content/ablution-cleansing-of-the-body-and-spirit-a133280

Chapter 7. Goat Grabbing and Kite Fighting
1. Afghan Embassy, Canberra, Australia: "Buzkashi" http://www.afghanembassy.net/buz.php

Chapter 8. Family Time
1. Max Planck Institute: "Textbook on Family Law in Afghanistan," October 19, 2010, http://www.mpipriv.de/ww/en/pub/research/research_work/foreign_law_comparative_law/islamic_legal_system/family_law_in_afghanistan.cfm
2. Catholic Relief Services, "Ensuring the Right to Education in Afghanistan," http://crs.org/afghanistan/education/
3. CIA—*The World Factbook:* "Afghanistan: Education," https://www.cia.gov/library/publications/the-world-factbook/geos/af.html

Books

Ali, Sharifah Enayat. *Afghanistan (Cultures of the World)*. Tarrytown, New York: Marshall Cavendish Books, 2006.

Gerber, Larry. *The Taliban in Afghanistan*. New York: Rosen Classroom, 2010.

Pohl, Kathleen. *Looking at Afghanistan*. New York: Gareth Stevens Publishing, 2008.

Sullivan, Michael P., and Tony O'Brien. *Afghan Dreams: Young Voices of Afghanistan*. New York: Bloomsbury USA Children's Books, 2008.

Whitehead, Kim. *Afghanistan*. Broomall, Pennsylvania: Mason Crest Publishers, 2009.

Whitfield, Susan. *Afghanistan (Countries of the World)*. Washington, DC: National Geographic Books, 2008.

Williams, Brian. *The War in Afghanistan*. New York: Franklin Watts, 2010.

Willis, Terri. *Afghanistan* (Enchantment of the World). New York: Scholastic Books, 2008.

Works Consulted

"Afghanistan: Landmine Fact Sheet," International Campaign to Ban Landmines, http://www.afghan-network.net/Landmines/

"Afghanistan's Environment 2008." United Nations Environment Programme. http://postconflict.unep.ch/publications/afg_soe_E.pdf

Bancroft, Peter. *Gem and Crystal Treasures*. Fallbrook, CA: Western Enterprises/Mineralogical Record, 1984; "Lapis Lazuli from Afghanistan" http://www.palagems.com/lapis_lazuli_bancroft.htm

Bonn-Muller, Eti. "Oldest Oil Paintings | Bamiyan, Afghanistan." *Archaeology,* Vol. 62, No. 1, January/February 2009. http://www.archaeology.org/0901/topten/oldest_oil_paintings.html

Clammer, Paul. *Lonely Planet Afghanistan*. Oakland, Calif.: Lonely Planet, 2007.

"The Destruction of the Statues in Bamiyan" http://www.photogrammetry.ethz.ch/research/bamiyan/buddha/destruction.html

Entezar, Ehsan. *Afghanistan 101*. Bloomington, Ind.: XLibris Corporation, 2010.

Harper, Jennifer. "Rare Bird Discovered in Afghan Mountains." *Washington Times,* January 15, 2010. http://www.washingtontimes.com/news/2010/jan/15/hidden-for-years-in-afghanistan-rare-bird-discover/

Irwin, Kristheena. "Ablution—Cleansing of the Body and Spirit." *Suite 101.com,* July 20, 2009. http://www.suite101.com/content/ablution-cleansing-of-the-body-and-spirit-a133280

Max Planck Institute: "Textbook on Family Law in Afghanistan," October 19, 2010. http://www.mpipriv.de/ww/en/pub/research/research_work/foreign_law_comparative_law/islamic_legal_system/family_law_in_afghanistan.cfm

Michaud, Roland and Sabrina. *Afghanistan: The Land That Was*. New York: Harry Abrams Publishing, 2002.

"Q&A: What Is a Loya Jirga?" *BBC News,* July 1, 2002. http://news.bbc.co.uk/2/hi/americas/1782079.stm

Rasanayagam, Angelo. *Afghanistan: A Modern History.* London, England: I. B. Tauris, 2005.

Reuters. "Nine Years On, The Taliban Have a Message for West." *Bernama,* November 15, 2010. http://www.bernama.com/bernama/v5/bm/newsworld.php?id=543158

Revkin, Andrew. "Afghanistan Protects 33 Species." Dot Earth, *The New York Times,* June 9, 2009. http://dotearth.blogs.nytimes.com/2009/06/09/afghanistan-protects-33-species/

Rotberg, Robert. *Building a New Afghanistan.* Washington. D.C.: Brookings Institution Press, 2007.

Runion, Meredith. *The History of Afghanistan.* Abingdon, Oxford: Greenwood, 2007.

Saberi, Helen. *Afghan Food and Cookery: Noshe Djan.* New York: Hippocrene Books, 2000.

Saikal, Amin. *Modern Afghanistan: A History of Struggle and Survival.* London, England: I.B. Tauris, 2006.

Tanner, Stephen. *Afghanistan: A Military History from Alexander the Great to the War Against the Taliban.* New York: Da Capo Press, 2009.

"What Is the Climate, Average Temperature/Weather in Afghanistan?" http://www.climatetemp.info/afghanistan/

On the Internet

Afghan Embassy, Canberra, Australia: Buzkashi
http://www.afghanembassy.net/buz.php

Afghanistan Culture
http://www.afghanistan-culture.com/

Afghanistan Travel
http://www.travelthewholeworld.com/afghanistan.html

CIA—*The World Factbook:* "Afghanistan"
https://www.cia.gov/library/publications/the-world-factbook/geos/af.html

Ministry of Foreign Affairs/Islamic Republic of Afghanistan
http://www.mfa.gov.af/afghanistan.asp

Revolutionary Association of the Women of Afghanistan
http://www.rawa.org/index.php

Tales of Asia: Afghanistan
http://www.talesofasia.com/afghanista.com

USAID: Afghanistan
http://afghanistan.usaid.gov/en/index.aspx

assassinate (uh-SAS-ih-nayt)—To murder for political reasons.

blasphemous (BLAS-feh-mus)—Lacking respect for what is considered sacred.

chaikhana (chay-KAH-nuh)—Any of the teahouses along the legendary Silk Road.

chapandaz (CHAP-un-dahz)—Master players of *buzkashi,* the national sport of Afghanistan.

drought (DROWT)—A long period with no rain that affects the water supply for drinking and crops.

fatwa (FAH-twah)—A ruling on a point of Islamic law from a recognized authority.

hajj (HAHJ)—The Islamic pilgrimage to Mecca.

idol—An image or other symbol that is worshiped.

jihad (jee-HOD)—Holy war.

jirga (JUR-guh)—A decision-making assembly of male elders.

Koran (kor-AN)—The Muslim holy book; also spelled *Qu'ran.*

Loya Jirga—"Grand council." A consultative assembly unique to Afghanistan in which, traditionally, tribal elders—Pashtuns, Tajiks, Hazaras, and Uzbeks—come together to settle affairs of the nation or to rally behind a cause.

minaret (MIN-uh-ret)—A tall, slender tower attached to a mosque.

mosque (MOSK)—A Muslim place of worship.

muezzin (moo-EH-zin)—A crier who calls from a tower the hour of prayer for Muslims.

mujahideen (moo-jah-hih-DEEN)—Muslim holy warriors involved in a jihad.

radical (RAD-ih-kul)—A member of a group who has extreme and strong viewpoints.

shah—A monarch by heredity.

shahadah (shah-HAH-dah)—The Muslim confession of faith.

shura (SHOO-rah)—Council.

Taliban (TAA-lih-ban)—A radical political group of the Middle East and especially Afghanistan.

Tamra Orr is a full-time writer and author living in the Pacific Northwest. She has traveled around the world through her interviews and research, and has written books about such fascinating countries as Indonesia, Brunei, Qatar, Bangladesh, and Turkey. Orr spends most of her time being a mother to four, a wife, an avid reader and researcher, and an eager armchair traveler.